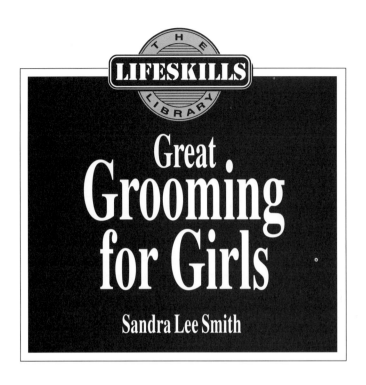

Great Grooming for Girls

Sandra Lee Smith

THE ROSEN PUBLISHING GROUP, INC.
NEW YORK

With love
To my sister Bonnie and her husband Richard,
the fashion trend-setters of our family.

Published in 1993 by The Rosen Publishing Group, Inc.
29 East 21st Street, New York, NY 10010

First Edition
Copyright 1993 by The Rosen Publishing Group, Inc.

Manufactured in the United States of America.

Library of Congress Cataloging-in-Publication Data

Smith, Sandra Lee.
    Great grooming for girls / Sandra Lee Smith.
        p.   cm. — (The Life skills library)
    Includes bibliographical references.
    Summary: Offers advice on making a good impression and discusses diet, exercise, hair care, make-up, and clothes.
    ISBN 0-8239-1469-0
    1. Grooming for girls—Juvenile literature. [1. Grooming.
2. Beauty, Personal.] I. Title II. Series.
RA777.25.S65 1993
646.7'046--dc20
                                      92-42113
                                          CIP
                                          AC

CONTENTS

FIRST IMPRESSIONS: THE OUTWARD APPEARANCE

How you look to others makes a statement about you. People can tell a lot about you from the first few minutes they see you. Just as you make judgments about the people you meet, people make judgments about you.

Imagine Martha, who is walking in a shopping mall. She sees some of her friends and other kids from school. As she walks along she suddenly sees a girl waving at her. It's her friend Susan. Martha starts to wave back until she notices who is with Susan. Stopping to stare, she can't believe her eyes.

Bright orange hair tied with at least twenty tiny ribbons. A pink blouse so big that it hangs to her knees. Baggy purple pants. Shoes that look like combat boots. Hot pink lipstick that is on crooked. Huge glasses practically an inch thick.

Good grooming requires a variety of "basic" hair, skin, and facial products.

Does Martha really want to meet this person? If she says "Hi," they may join her. And what if the boys see her with a girl who looks so silly? Then again, she doesn't want to hurt Susan's feelings.

The girl's looks make Martha think twice about being with her. Martha waves and slips into the nearest store to avoid them. They go on by, and Martha continues her stroll down the mall. Soon she hears someone calling. She looks around, and there is her cousin. Clinging to him is a girl wearing skin-tight jeans, a low-cut tank top, dangling earrings, and heavy makeup. This isn't the type of girl he usually dates. Martha doesn't want to be seen with them either, so she waves and moves along.

After she passes two more stores, Martha sees her friends Rhonda and Lisa. They are dressed much the same as Martha. They are just strolling much the way Martha is. She hurries to catch up with them and join them for the day.

A Matter of Appearance

Can you see how appearances shaped Martha's social contacts? It is natural to use first impressions to decide whom you want to be with. However, it is important not to make snap judgments.

Think about all the people you know. Do you remember the first time you saw them? Can you recall what they were wearing? What you thought about them? Did you know at once whether you liked them or not?

The first contact with another person makes a big impression on us. In those first few minutes we make many decisions. We look at styles of clothing. We talk and think maybe we could be friends. We decide whether this person will fit in with our other friends. Or perhaps we think we don't ever want this person as a friend.

Sometimes we make quick decisions about people to protect ourselves. A stranger we meet in a public place could be very dangerous. How the person is dressed may give us a clue. For example, if you meet a strange boy in the park who is dressed like a gang member, you will probably not want to stop and talk with him.

Another reason we check people out is to keep our lives in order. We meet so many people that we need to pick and choose which ones we will get to know. To find out who would be best to talk to or be with, we have learned to make judgments about people.

Our first judgment is based on our senses: what we see, hear, and smell. Suppose you need somebody to study with. Your teacher introduces you to Jerrie. If you come close to Jerrie and smell heavy perfume, you may decide you don't want to be stuck in a small study room with her.

We've all learned that snap judgments are not always true. You may need more information to make better decisions. But, it is easy to make snap judgments. And because of that, you need to pay close attention to how *you* appear.

First Impressions

If someone were to meet you for the first time, what would they be able to tell about you? Are you neat and tidy? Or are you dirty and sloppy? Do you have any fashion sense? Are your clothes right for the occasion? Are you involved in a cult group or a gang? Are you with the "in" crowd?

Your appearance can also tell about your interests. If you wear jeans and boots and your skin is sun-tanned, one can figure that you like the outdoors. If you are wearing the latest style of a hot rock group, one can guess that you like that kind of music.

Your appearance makes a statement about who you are. If you are a person who loves volunteering in a hospital or in your religious organization, you do not want to wear clothes that make you look as if you just came off the playing field or track.

If you are at the mall and want to meet boys, it would be wise to take care how you dress. A tight sweater and short, short skirt may invite the wrong kind of boy.

There are many things to think about when planning your appearance. Are the colors and styles you wear the best for your body? Is your hairstyle the best for your face? Are you healthy, and do you look it? If you don't take note of how you look, no one else will either.

CHAPTER
2

SECOND IMPRESSIONS: THE "INNER YOU"

Of all the things you wear, your expression is the most important. When people get past the first impression, they begin to notice the "inner you." From this impression they will decide whether or not they want to know you. You, too, go beyond outward looks when you meet people and start to find out what they really are like.

Let's go back to the mall. Rhonda and Lisa were dressed like Martha, so they passed the first impression test. But after a few minutes, Martha begins to form her second impressions.

"Did you see Susan?" asks Rhonda.

"Who was that with her?" Martha asks.

"I don't know," Lisa laughs, "and I don't want to know. Anyone who looks that weird must be a real loser."

"Could be," Martha agrees. "I'm glad I found you two."

"Let's go look at necklaces," Rhonda says, pointing to a store display. At the counter, Martha picks up one she likes.

Lisa suddenly grabs it. "You don't want that! It's the ugliest thing I've ever seen."

"Where's your taste, girl?" Rhonda holds up another chain. "Isn't this gross?"

"Yuk," Lisa agrees. "Let's go somewhere else. They don't have anything here."

Martha walks through several more stores as Lisa and Rhonda pick apart everything they see. They never have a good word to say. Suddenly Martha spots Susan and her strange companion. Martha waves. At least Susan says funny things.

Rhonda pulls Martha close to her. "Don't talk to them. They might come over here."

"Susan's okay," Martha says.

Lisa cuts in, "Do you mean Miss Suzy Perfect?"

"Susan's lots of fun," Martha says. "Anyway, I need to tell her something."

"Go ahead," Rhonda says as she backs up and grabs Lisa. "We're out of here."

Then Susan comes up to Martha and says, "Hi. This is my cousin, Laura. She's been doing a clown display for the kids in the toy store. Doesn't she look wild?"

Martha smiles, liking the girl already. "I bet you're real popular with them," Martha says.

—

Your appearance "says" a lot about you.

Meeting the "Inner You"

Laura did not make a good first impression, but she did make a much better second impression than Rhonda or Lisa did. Martha discovered that attitude makes up a big part of your overall appearance. Meeting a person with a beautiful face, perfect figure, and stylish clothes will not make a good impression if she is always angry or negative.

In the same way, someone who looks a little different may have a wonderful personality. Martha soon changed her first impression of Susan's cousin after she was introduced.

Your looks are affected by your speech. Swearing or saying unkind things can make a beautiful person seem unattractive. Your words reflect the inner you.

What if you had an important job interview? You would want to present yourself in the best possible way. You would dress carefully, and fix your hair and makeup. To complete the picture, you would need to have a confident and pleasant attitude.

Employers want to hire people who are friendly, confident, and bright. You need to convey a likable personality along with an appealing appearance.

The same ideas apply when going out on a date. A boy may ask a girl out because of her attractive appearance, but whether or not he asks her for a second date depends upon the inner person.

Your inner attitude also affects how you feel. And we'll see in the next chapter how important good health is to your looks.

YOU ARE WHAT YOU EAT

Health and diet play important roles in how you look. Physical features help, that is true. It is nice to have smooth skin. It is good to have pretty teeth, an attractive smile, beautiful eyes. These wonderful features can be to your advantage if you keep them that way by staying healthy.

Even if your features are not striking, but are average or plain, they can be enhanced by health. When you eat the right foods, your hair stays shiny. The right foods help to keep your skin free of blemishes. Proper diet gives you the best figure you can attain with your body build.

Even a pretty girl does not look well if she is sick. A body has no appeal if it is undernourished. You cannot wear a smile and have a bubbly personality if you don't feel well.

Diet Is Not Only for Reducing

Scientists and doctors are proving more and more how a good diet improves health. People who eat too many fats and sweets can have heart problems. People who smoke have lung and breathing problems. People who abuse alcohol or drugs destroy brain tissue. These problems may seem far off because it may take a lot of abuse before they show up. Our bodies have the ability to make up for some of the things we do to them. When we are young we think we can get away with more.

Don't kid yourself into thinking that diet is something to worry about when you are older, or only if you are overweight. Diet should be everyone's daily concern.

The human body does best when it is fed well. There are many books in the library or bookstores that give good advice on what to eat. We are not talking about fad diets, but good eating habits.

High-fiber, low-fat diets are favored by most scientists and doctors. Foods high in fiber include grains such as rice, whole wheat, barley, corn, oats, and rye. Our bodies also require plenty of fruits and vegetables. Leafy green vegetables are best for us. Proteins are necessary, but they can be obtained from many sources other than fatty meats. Beans and rice are great sources of protein.

Eating habits are just that—*habits*. Habits are patterns of behavior that are set after repeated use.

—

A healthy diet is important to keep you looking and feeling your best.

Making an effort to eat healthful foods as often as possible will help you to develop good eating habits. If you are hungry for something sweet, get in the habit of having fruit instead of cake or candy. For a snack, try popcorn instead of chips. Instead of beef, try fish and poultry.

A good general rule to keep in mind is that anything containing fat will turn into fat on your body. Or it will turn into oily skin or pimples and blemishes. Every time you bite into a big hunk of cheese, picture where it is going to end up. Do the same for chocolate candy, which is mostly fat, or ice cream, french fries, or chips.

In the same manner, picture how grains such as rice, whole wheat, and oatmeal are going through your body like tiny vacuum cleaners, picking up all the bad things and cleaning you out. Fruit and vegetables act the same way.

It helps to drink plenty of fluids. Water is best. It acts to cleanse your tissues. Fruit juices are good if they are natural, with no added sugar. Milk is good in small quantities. Remember the fat content. If you can, drink low-fat milk.

Sodas, coffee, tea, and other artificial drinks may contain many harmful chemicals.

Watch Out for Legal and Illegal Drugs

Putting poisons in your body is especially bad for your health and your looks. Poisons in your body cause stress. Doctors and scientists have shown that alcohol is a poison. It damages your liver, which is the organ that keeps your blood clean.

Other drugs are more damaging. Using them sometimes causes people not to eat at all. They can suffer from malnutrition. They pick up illnesses easily because their immune system is not in good working order.

Looks are more than just physical features. You can take advantage of your looks by eating healthy foods. You can make your body look its best by giving it the best possible foods.

CHAPTER 4

KEEPING FIT

In the last chapter we discussed the importance of health to your beauty and looks. Linked to good health is proper exercise. Keeping fit not only keeps your body in good working order, but it relieves stress and keeps your mind and emotions healthy.

Movie stars depend upon their looks for their jobs and their stardom. Because their looks are so important to them, they end up spending many hours a week and thousands of dollars to exercise and stay fit. Their routine is extreme. We don't all need to pay as much attention to our looks as a movie star does. But we can learn some important lessons from the stars in regard to beauty and good looks.

Most models and stars need to have perfect bodies. Athletes and others who use their bodies for

Regular exercise keeps you physically fit and mentally alert.

survival, such as the men and women of the armed forces, also focus on keeping their bodies fit. They do this first by proper diet, which we discussed in the last chapter. Athletes and people who do extensive exercise need to eat more food than normal. They need more protein and fats than most teens do.

If you are on a heavy exercise schedule, you need to eat accordingly. Most athletes have trainers or coaches who advise them on what to eat and how much exercise to take. It is best to have an adviser or trainer if you are working out especially hard. Too much exercise can be just as harmful to your body as too little.

Most of us, however, do best with a fair amount of exercise each day. If you take physical education in school, you probably get what you need. During the summer and on weekends, you need to provide your own program of exercise.

There are many books on proper exercise. Most common are the aerobic exercises. These include walking, jogging, running, bicycling, and swimming. Done in moderation, these forms of exercise provide the best overall program. Exercises such as sit-ups, leg lifts, push-ups, and weight lifting help to build up certain areas of your body.

Improving on Nature

To focus on problem areas, you can do individual exercises. Magazines have articles that give hints on trimming thighs, waists, and hips. They suggest exercises for building breasts and arms. Videos that you can check out of the library or buy demonstrate well-rounded exercise programs. These are also fun because they have lively music to work out with.

All of these workouts serve to improve your body. That is why movie stars and models pay so much attention to their exercise. It enhances their looks. It takes what features they have and improves them.

Exercise can also improve a poor body build. Some exercises help to build muscles, or add body bulk. Others take off inches or tone down features you don't want noticed.

To be effective, exercise must be done on a regular basis. That can become boring and tiresome. It helps to vary the exercises you do. Perhaps you can do aerobic exercises every other day and do body-building exercises in between. Exercising does not have to become tiresome. Many forms of exercise are entertaining.

Dancing is an excellent aerobic exercise and is fun besides. You must be careful, however, not to defeat your purpose by dancing in an unhealthy place. A good workout makes you breathe heavily because you need more oxygen. Where there is a lot of cigarette smoke, your body takes in poison when it needs pure air the most. Extended dancing burns calories. However, if you are using alcohol or other drugs your energy is not being used to build healthy muscles and tissue, but to clean out the poison.

Many teen centers, religious organizations, and community centers provide dances for teens that are

Taking care of yourself builds confidence.

fun and healthful. Not only do they help you get aerobic exercise, they also provide you with a place where you can meet new friends.

There are many ways to get exercise without its becoming drudgery. Team play offers fun along with the exercise. Volleyball, badminton, tennis, basketball, swimming, and soccer are all sports that require aerobic exercise. Skiing, ice skating, and sledding are all fun winter sports that give you a chance to exercise outdoors—even in cold weather.

In some cities, shopping malls open early to walkers, who take advantage of the level floors and safety to get their exercise. Many communities have gymnasiums that offer aerobic exercise programs. The gyms often have advisers who will help you select exercises that are right for you.

If possible, it is best to get your exercise outdoors. Something about the clear air and getting in touch with nature cleanses the mind and soul as well as the body. Most cities have parks. If you live in the country there are roads and paths you can take. Be sure to let your family know where you are, and be sure to choose safe places to exercise.

Exercising makes you take in more oxygen. It makes your blood flow more freely. That is what cleanses your body. By exercising regularly, you put your blood through a filtering process that removes harmful waste particles from your system. It brings in the clean oxygen your body needs to work properly. That is why people who exercise are healthier.

Relying on natural looks can be very deceptive. It is wonderful if you have natural beauty. But it is also your responsibility to keep it. If you don't think you are that beautiful, there are many ways to bring out the beauty within you. Everyone has something that makes her unique and special. Proper exercise helps that special quality to shine through. People are often attracted to the health and vibrancy that come from a fit and healthy body.

If you do need to shampoo often, pay attention to the condition of your hair. Too much washing can cause your hair to become dry and brittle. You may need to find a gentler shampoo or find a rinse or treatment that will restore the natural oils.

Types of Hair

People have different types of hair. Some have thick and oily hair. Others have thin or dry hair. Read the labels on shampoos to find out which is best for your type of hair. It is also wise to read labels to find out exactly what you are putting on your hair. Some products contain wax that builds up on your hair and can ruin it. Others contain harsh chemicals.

People who are allergic to perfumes should find unscented products. It is nice to have perfumed hair, but it is better to have a clear skin and scalp. If a product makes your scalp itch or your hair fall out, stop using it right away.

Many products on the market can make your hair more beautiful. Try some of them and find what works best for you. Mousse can give more body to your hair. Care is needed with it because extended use can cause skin irritation.

Hair sprays have been in use for many years. Unscented brands are usually not harmful to your hair or to your skin. It is best to cover your face with a cloth or tissue before applying the spray, as it coats your skin as well as your hair and prevents your pores from breathing properly. If you are concerned about air pollution, avoid aerosol hair sprays that contain harmful chemicals. Pump sprays are available that are just as effective.

Creme rinses and conditioners help to repair hair damaged from perms or coloring. They also help in combing out wet, tangled hair and make it easier to style. If you blow-dry your hair every day, you might consider these items. Hot air does damage your hair. It causes split ends and dries out the natural oils in your hair.

Coloring and Perms

Hair coloring and perms can enhance your looks, but they can also harm your hair. Many products contain strong chemicals. When coloring your hair, also be sure to consider how the shade will look with your skin tone. Sometimes lighter hair color can make a girl look pale.

In the same way, a person with light hair and skin may look strange with very dark hair.

Most people tint their hair to shades that are close to their natural color. For example, if you have a mousy shade of brown hair, you can lighten it to an ash blonde or darken it slightly to a richer brown, or perhaps add reddish tints to it. Another advantage to choosing a shade close to your own color is that differences in color are not as noticeable when your hair starts growing out. This is important to consider because it is not wise to color your hair more often than every two months.

Perms are wonderful if you can wear them. They are especially helpful for the active teen who doesn't want to spend hours in front of the mirror but still wants to look nice. Perms at beauty salons are quite expensive. If you have a friend or relative to help you, it is very inexpensive to do your own perm. It can also be healthier because you can control the time better and avoid burning your hair.

Because of the strong chemicals in perm solutions, it is wise to follow instructions carefully and to test the product on a bit of your hair before actually applying it. It takes months for a perm to grow out, so you want to be sure you have what

—

Experimenting with makeup will help you to find the look that's right for you.

you want. Beauticians can help you select a perm. A good beauty supply store will also have people who can answer your questions.

Hair Styles

To make the most of your looks, it is important to choose a hair style that suits your face. It is nice to be in fashion, but that may not flatter you at all. It would be better to wear a style that makes the most of your looks.

Length of hair is an important factor. Some girls look wonderful with long flowing hair. Others, however, look better with short or medium-length hair. It depends on your body build and the shape of your face. A hair stylist can help you select your best style. But it is often easier and less expensive to experiment yourself.

There are some general rules to consider. If your face is long and narrow, a shorter, fluffier hair style may look best. It can add fullness to your face. Someone with a round or squared face, however, can wear her hair long and straight. If you have a full face, avoid the short curly styles. Try medium or longer styles, and keep the sides brushed back. A short close cut would also be attractive.

Hair styles can be made to look exciting and different by using bows, clips, or scarves. Be creative and discover a look that fits you. Choose bright colors that will bring out your natural beauty.

DETAILS YOU CAN CHANGE

Most of us have to live with the features we were born with. Some things cannot be changed, but certain details can be easily altered to make one more attractive. For example, you cannot change the overall tone of your skin. You may have an olive tone, a peach tone, or a chocolate brown tone. You can, however, change the shade. Your skin will darken when you expose it to sunlight or man-made ultraviolet rays. It will lighten if you stay protected from the sun.

Skin care can make a big difference in how you look. Makeup and cream products are available to keep your skin beautiful. If you have blemishes, you can cover them with makeup. If you have dry, cracked skin, it can be softened with creams.

Good grooming means making the most of what you have.

Your skin will be more glowing and healthy if you keep it clean. Many soaps and cleansing products on the market are designed to keep that fresh look. Prices vary, but price is not the only difference. Check the ingredients. Be careful about products having too much perfume or fragrance. They can cause blemishes and skin rashes.

Find a makeup dealer (like Mary Kay or Nu Skin) to help you select the best products for your skin. These experts can help you choose the colors that are best for you. They can show you how to apply eye shadow and mascara and to choose the best lipstick colors.

If you cannot afford a specialist, go to a local department store and let the clerks show you their products. Often name-brand makeup companies have demonstrators who give advice as part of their sales effort. There is no obligation to buy.

It is somewhat risky to experiment with makeup. You can end up looking strange if you put makeup on wrong. You can also damage your skin with products that are not made for facial skin.

Sometimes it is "in" to mark your skin with fake moles or beauty spots or to put designs on your skin. Remember that these fashion fads do not last long. Be careful about tattoos. They are on your skin forever. If you get a tattoo because it is the fad today, you may be sorry later on in life when it is no longer popular. You can achieve the same look with stickers and inks, which can be removed when the fad has run its course.

Your Body Skin

It is also important to keep your body skin in good shape. Cleanliness is the most important factor. It is wise to bathe at least two or three times a week, depending upon your life-style. If you are active in sports, you need to bathe daily.

Because your skin produces natural oils for its protection, you need to use soaps and cleansers to clean it properly. Just rinsing in water will not cut the build-up of oils. These oils and the moisture that comes from sweat glands will cause your body to have bad odors.

Deodorants are very helpful in controlling body odors. Antiperspirants work best, but they must be used with care. They are strong and can cause an allergic reaction on delicate skin.

The oils and sweat that cause body odors are transmitted to your clothing, causing odors there, too. Warm water and detergents dissolve oils. You might prefer to buy clothes that can be washed rather than those that need dry cleaning.

Scents

Perfumes can help you smell fresh. Perfumes are like fashion and clothes: The different scents define who you are. Therefore it is wise to try several perfumes and choose those that fit your personality. If you like the outdoors, you might like a light woodsy scent for the daytime.

Perfumes, like makeup, contain chemicals. Be sure to try them on the inside of your arm or knee where the skin doesn't show. Many girls are allergic to the ingredients of perfumes. You want to be sure you won't have an allergic reaction before you put perfume on skin that shows. Also beware of wearing perfume before sunbathing. Some chemicals react to the ultraviolet rays of the sun.

Perfumes work best when used on the parts of your body that stay warm. The most common areas are your wrists, elbows, knees, temples, and behind your ears. You might want to wear different scents depending on the occasion: lighter in the day, heavier for the evening.

There are many types of scents. Perfume is the strongest, then cologne, and then toilet water. Bath oils, shower gels, bubble baths, powders, and creams are other ways to scent your body.

Smile!

Your smile is one of your best features. Therefore it is important to keep your teeth looking beautiful. Food trapped in your teeth not only is unattractive but causes breath odor. Your dentist can show you how to care properly for your teeth and gums.

Crooked teeth and badly stained teeth are things we do not have to live with today. Orthodontists can straighten teeth. Dentists have brighteners to whiten teeth. These processes are expensive but worth the money. Beautiful teeth are for a lifetime.

Nail Enhancement

Finally, you can enhance your appearance with proper nail care of your hands and feet. Your hands are always in public view. Professional manicurists can show you how to shape and polish your nails. Learning to take care of them yourself is the easiest way to keep nails healthy and beautiful.

As with makeup and perfumes, try different products. Some contain chemicals that will damage your nails if you are allergic to them. Be careful with false nails. They can make a stunning improvement; but, extensive use of them can destroy the natural nail underneath.

Diet can improve the quality of your nails. Calcium-rich foods, for example, will help make nails stronger. Their appearance also depends upon habits. If you bite or chew on your cuticles and nails, you need to change your habits. Weekly care with proper equipment such as nail file, pumice stone, orange stick, and buffer will transform your nails into an attractive asset.

No matter what your diet or habits, you should keep your nails clean. Germs can collect under toenails and fingernails, causing odors, infections, and fungal diseases.

Learn to select the colors of nail polish that go best with your skin tone and the clothes you wear. Dark-colored polish tends to show chipping more than light colors. Think about decorating your fingernails with designs, jewels, or glitter.

CLOTHES THAT ARE YOU

Fashion can be tricky because the fads and styles are always changing. However, there are a few basics that will help you to select and maintain the best possible wardrobe. Fads do change from season to season. Styles and colors come and go. What helps in setting up your wardrobe is knowing what image you wish to portray. It also helps to understand your life-style so you can live and dress according to what is best for you.

In spite of fads, basics stay in style through most changes. The basic colors are black, brown, and navy blue. Every person looks best in one of those colors. If you design your wardrobe around one basic color, you can mix and match to save money and have more outfits to wear. For example, if you

The right accessories can give a brand-new look to an old outfit.

have black dress shoes, casual shoes, and tennis shoes, you can wear them with all your outfits that are basic black, or colors that go with those that feature black.

A simple skirt or dress and a pair of pants in your basic color can be mixed and matched with several bright-colored tops or sweaters. You won't need many pairs of shoes and purses if they are also in your basic color. Coats and jackets can go with all your clothes if you keep them in the basic color.

Selecting colors that coordinate is important. You want them to go with your basic color. For example, if your basic color is brown, you will want other colors that go well with brown, such as ivory and gold, teal blue, olive green, peach, and dusty rose. Colors that go well with black are bright white, blood red, fuschia, bright blues and greens, and orange. Navy blue looks well with red, whites, shades of blue, yellow, pale pink, and beige.

Flatter Yourself

Select the range of colors that flatter your skin. Department stores and some fashion sales clerks offer *colorizing*. This is simply a process of choosing the colors that look best on you. It can be expensive, but in the long run you will save quite a bit of money because you won't waste it on clothes you will never wear.

In general, women of color wear winter or summer colors that are based on black and navy blue.

Light-skinned women often wear spring or autumn colors that are based on the browns and blues. This is not a hard-and-fast rule; it is best to have your skin analyzed by the experts.

Decide on a Basic Style

Once color is decided, it is wise to find out what style looks best on you. There are several basic styles. Tailored clothes include tweeds, plaids, and suits. Some girls look better in the frills and lace of a more feminine style.

Once you have determined the basics, you can branch out to make your fashion statement. If you are an outdoors woman, choose fashions that suit that life-style. If you go to lots of dances, find clothes within the basics that are good to dance in. If you enjoy parties, buy outfits that can be worn at parties and also at school or elsewhere. If you have a job, you need to dress for it.

Match Style to Figure

Consider your body shape when selecting clothes. If you have a long, thin body, stay away from narrow skirts and straight jackets, which will make you look longer and thinner. Full skirts, baggy pants, and loose blouses will flatter your figure nicely. If you are short and round, perhaps overweight, narrow skirts and straight jackets will work out best for you. Just remember to keep it simple.

Again, look in the mirror or get together with friends who will be honest and decide on styles that flatter your body. While you are at it, try varied fabrics and patterns. Do you look better in plaids, stripes, prints, paisleys, or solid colors? The designs and prints affect your figure and the way it looks. Vertical stripes draw the eye upward and enhance the thin, tall look. Stripes going across the body add width to your body. If you are thin, adding width will be an advantage. If you are heavy, you will want to stay away from that look.

After colors, style, fabrics, and your life-style have been considered, you can buy your basics. In order to enhance the distinctive look that is *you*, you must take the time to choose the best possible accessories. Jewelry can turn a basic dress into a party dress. A colorful scarf can turn a plain skirt and blouse into a stunning outfit. A hat can give you a business look or a festive look, depending on the style.

The best way to get ideas for accessories is to glance through fashion magazines and see how the models are dressed. When you go out shopping, look at the models in the store windows. Fashion designers are trained to make the most out of clothes. They work hard to make attractive outfits to put on display. Notice how they add the accessories. When you go shopping, wear a basic outfit and try on various items with it. You will be surprised how many different combinations you can make out of one basic outfit.

SHOPPING TIPS

Now that you know what styles and colors are best for you, it is time to shop for your clothes. You need to buy the basics first. Find a good basic skirt, pants, and dress. You also need to buy shoes, purses, and a coat. For your basics, it is wise to buy quality clothes.

Quality clothes do not necessarily have to be expensive. You can find them on sale. If you sew well, you can make them with good-quality fabrics. When it comes to extra blouses and accessories, you can be more flexible and take advantage of discount stores and low-cost warehouses. It is especially wise to pay less when you are buying a fad item, because it won't stay in style long.

Quality clothes last longer and come out of the wash or dry cleaner still looking well. Colors remain true and fabrics stay crisp.

Buying on a Budget

Most teens have a clothing budget. If you don't, it would be wise to think about one. Once in the store, it is easy to be tempted into buying things you do not need, or spending too much money and not ending up with what you wanted.

Store managers pay experts to decorate their stores in a way that makes you want to buy everything you see. Next time you go into a store, notice what is placed near the doors and in the aisles. You will see styles that are the latest fashion. Bright colors flash out at you. The most expensive items are displayed first so that you will buy them instead of the inexpensive items you came in for.

To make the most of your budget and to acquire the wardrobe that is you, plan ahead. Make a list of what you need. Then list the things you want. Keep in mind how much money you have to spend, and then shop for the items. At the store, go directly to the department and bypass the displays. Make your purchases and leave.

If you want to window-shop to see what styles are in, do that on another trip—or at least after you have made your purchases. That way you will not spend your budgeted money on unplanned items. And you will not waste time. Window-shopping is fun, but it can make you too tired to shop for what you really need.

—
Careful shopping allows you to buy the clothes you want at prices you can afford.

Bargain Hunting

Many teens stretch their dollars by shopping in secondhand stores or at garage sales. Discount warehouses often have name brands at lower prices. Some stores have a section for damaged clothes that are marked down. If you are an expert at sewing, you can often fix the outfit and end up with a high-quality garment for less money.

Buying out of season is another way to make the most of your budget, especially when shopping for basics. At the end of each season, stores want to put out their new lines. They sell the leftovers at great bargain prices.

Care is also needed when shopping for these bargains. Something may look great and be at a low price, but if it is not within your color scheme or style you can waste even that small amount of money. Be sure it fits into your plan.

There is one easy rule when shopping—*When in doubt, leave it out.* If you aren't sure, go home and think about it. Some sales clerks are such experts at talking you into buying that you may purchase an outfit you know isn't quite right.

Everyone makes mistakes when shopping. For one thing, colors often don't look true under the store lighting. When you get home, try the outfit on again; if it is not what you really want, take it back while you can. Don't clutter your closet with clothes you will never wear when you can fill it instead with outfits that are perfect for you.

GLOSSARY
EXPLAINING NEW WORDS

accessory Something added to an outfit to make it complete, or give it a new look.

aerobic exercise Exercise that brings oxygen into the blood.

allergy Reaction to a substance.

antiperspirant Substance that reduces perspiration or sweating.

attitude A mental position or feeling in regard to an object or person.

colorizing Matching colors to skin tones.

confidence A state of trust or intimacy.

consultant One whom you ask for advice or an opinion.

gymnasium A place for indoor sport activities.

immunity A state of being exempt.

impression An opinion resulting from influence.

judgment Process of forming an opinion.

orthodontist A dental specialist who straightens teeth.

personality Personal and social traits of a person.

professional A trained person who does something with great skill.

stress A factor that creates bodily tension.

tresses Long locks of hair.

ultraviolet Rays from the sun that produce radiation.

wardrobe A collection of clothes.

FOR FURTHER READING

Magazines

Teen Magazine, Harper's Bazaar, Ebony, Mademoiselle, Seventeen, Ladies' Home Journal, Essence, Weight Watchers Magazine, Woman's Day, Good Housekeeping, Redbook, Vogue

Nonfiction Teens

Saunders, Rubie. *Good Grooming for Girls.* New York: Franklin Watts, 1976.

Zeldis, Vona. *Coping with Beauty, Fitness and Fashion.* New York: Rosen Publishing Group, 1987.

Nonfiction Adult

Berenson, Marisa. *Dressing Up—How to Look and Feel Absolutely Perfect for Any Social Occasion.* New York: G.P. Putnam's sons, 1984.

Chaffee, Suzy, and Adler, Bill. *The I Love My Fitness Book.* New York: William Morrow and Company, 1983.

Jackson, Carole. *Color Me Beautiful: Discover Your Natural Beauty Through the Colors That Make You Look Great.* Washington, D.C.: Acropolis Books, Ltd., 1984.

Kingsley, Philip. *The Complete Hair Book.* New York: Grosset & Dunlap, 1979.

Revelli, Clare. *Style and You: Every Woman's Guide to Total Style.* New York: Pocket Books, 1989.

Walden, Barbara. *Easy Glamour: The Black Woman's Definitive Guide to Beauty and Style.* New York: William Morrow and Co., 1981.

INDEX

47

About the Author

For twenty-one years, Sandra Lee Smith has taught grades from kindergarten through college level in California and Arizona.

Active on legislative committees and in community projects, she helped design programs to involve parents in the education process.

In response to the President's Report, *A Nation at Risk*, Ms. Smith participated in a project involving Arizona State University, Phoenix Elementary School District, and an inner-city community in Phoenix. Participants in the project developed a holistic approach to education.

Photo Credits

All photos on cover and in book by Dru Nadler except p.28, Chris Volpe.

Design & Production: Blackbirch Graphics, Inc.